Waco Cultural Arts Fest

WordFest Anthology 2020

Edited by
Sandi Horton

Waco Cultural Arts Fest: WordFest Anthology 2020

Copyright ©2020

All rights revert to the individual authors, artists, and editors.

ISBN: 9798666626559

Cover Art: *"I Feel You"*, 24 X 30, oil on canvas

Artist: Charles Wallis is a graduate of the Baylor
University fine art program. He is a master painter and
versatile in many mediums and styles. He paints
primarily modern impressionist and abstract pieces.

Artist Statement:
My art is an expression of my spirit to the spirit of others that
connect with it. I seek to create a memory, a wish, a fantasy
or moment of joy or peace in the soul of the viewer. I pursue
ideas, color combinations or images that attract my attention.

Artist description of cover art *"I Feel You"*

Empathetic or sensitive people often feel the emotions of those
around them.
They sometimes have difficulty distinguishing group thought
and feeling from their own. Just as some have better eye sight
or hearing than normal, some people have more highly
developed central nervous systems than normal which picks
up more information from their environment. This is about
20% of the population. This can create a need to 'get away' to
sort things out.
They rely on their intuition for primary guidance in their
everyday life.
This combination of being highly sensitive and relying on
intuition exists in these people in varying degrees of intensity.

From the editor of *WordFest Anthology 2020*

This is the fifth anthology I have compiled and edited for
the Waco Cultural Arts Fest – WordFest. Producing this
book is a labor of love for the poets and their poems
featured in this anthology. The poems are published as
they are submitted.

The 2020 WordFest Anthology recognizes U.S. poets
from Texas, California, New York, Michigan, North
Carolina, Arkansas, Pennsylvania, Washington,
Wisconsin, Rhode Island, Oklahoma, Hawaii, Illinois,
Michigan, Oregon, and New Jersey. International poets
represent India, Kenya, and the United Kingdom.

This diverse collection of 21st century poems will give
readers a new way to think about our theme of 'fire'.

The uncertainty of regulations by state and local officials,
due to the COVID-19 pandemic, are preventing the
publication of the 2020 WordFest Schedule. We are
tentatively planning to meet in person at the Waco
Convention Center as part of a smaller scale Waco
Cultural Arts Fest the first week-end of October. One of
the highlights of our festival is the annual anthology
reading and the distribution of books to those reading.
Also this year, we are planning a workshop and a reading
by the *Texas Poetry Calendar 2021* writers and editors.
Steve Sanders plans to be on hand to make professional
recordings for attending poets. Michael Guinn plans to
host our open mics and readings. The Heart of Texas
Native American Style Flute Circle may also return to
participate in a blending of music and poetry.

I look forward to seeing and hearing a variety of poets at
the 2020 WordFest!

Sandi Horton

71 S. Rupsha Mitra	"Autumn Fire"
72 Kayla Mize	"Diminish"
73 Susan Munsch	"Fire Flies at the Balloon Fiesta"
74 Tom Murphy	"May Fire"
75 Ann Marie Newman	"I Am Drama Darlin'"
76 Otieno Lawi Ondiek	"It's Called … Fire"
77 Michael Owens	"Almost Unnoticed"
78 Christa Pandey	"Ravaged"
79 Alice Parker	"A Comfy Chair"
80 Juan M. Perez	"Flame: A Zombie Zonnet"
81 DaRell Pittman	"House Fire"
82 Gerald Plant	"Fire Watcher"
83 Jiaan Powers	"Dark Night"
84 Betty Roberts	"A Prayer for These Pandemic Times"
85 Irene C. Robertson	"The Holocaust of a Disease"
86 Susan J. Rogers	"Lifetime of Desire"
87 Barry Rynk	"Frederick's Fire"
88 Cindye Sablatura	"Revelation"
89 Kathryn Sadakierski	"Faith is the Fire"
90 Steve Sanders	"Fire for a Change"

Discovering Leontyne Price

Midnight - my sister bending
over her mother's shoulder
whispering to wake her

they tiptoed to the family's ancient
tube radio - listened to music
via waves north across the Alps

from La Scala in Milan
to a mesmerizing understudy
a voice of bell-like clarity

a first on-stage performance
in the Fall of 1957 left them speechless –
winging on unsteady radio waves

unhurried - distinct - reassuring
honey and velvet
Mein Gott, wer ist denn das? who is she?

they shivered in midnight chill
straining to follow Leontyne Price
singing Verdi's *Aida*

and news of a young American phenomenon
spread like wildfire through a stunned world
of Europe's opera fans

Kaye Voigt Abikhaled
Austin, Texas

Mouth of Fire

I do nothing here but come undone
in this whirlwind of seconds:
thread, this pulse of mine, of time that threads us:
eager time, mouth of fire
where history burns and burns again
in an endless conflagration.

At the end of every moment
I rescue the ashes that I become
where I will be born again
birthed from death
on the threshold of the moments to come.

Time blazes on itself;
and in its everlasting flame
blaze that devours everything
and turns it into dust of nothingness
spring of shadows
death revives us
perpetual, simmering.

Julio César Aguilar
Waco, Texas

Rage

We have this fire
deep inside
We forget it exists
but it does live,
an ancient dragon in slumber

We are fearful
to wake this dragon
but sometimes we get careless

It has been ages
since this dragon
even opened its eyes

Is it a myth?
Merely to scare little children

No, be careful
It is real

Guard yourself
and your loved ones
from this dragon

Be vigilant!
Don't let the kindling of anger
become the inferno of rage

Let the dragon sleep
otherwise your village will burn

Tarik Ahmed
Allen, Texas

A Grudge

There is a fire inside me
That is fueled by anger

It grows bigger
Whenever I see laughter
In who hurt me

Their breath
Their walk
Just the sight of them
Fuels this fire

It makes life harder on me

Have come to realize that
The only way to put out this fire
Is to forgive
Because this grudge
Is burning no one
But me

Serene Abu Anbar
McKinney, Texas

Every Winter Morning

The scrape of the tin shovel across brick
greeted me in the darkness while I lay curled,
warm beneath the old patchwork quilt,
the one with two tiny pieces of green satin
and two small squares of worn purple velvet,
pieced long, long ago by Miss Jule's mama.

I lay dozing while *my* Mama worked,
shoveling yesterday's ash, preparing the way
for today's comfort, crumpling old news
into clusters of fuel, re-purposed for the cause
and placed with intent beneath the grate,
the empty cradle begging to be filled.

With delicate determination, Mama placed the
kindling into those waiting metal arms with an
artistic eye, the way she decorated a cake.
The final touch was transferred, chunk by chunk,
from the ancient iron cauldron,
as black as the coal it protected.

The strike of the match flashed in semidarkness.
Match burns paper, paper burns kindling,
kindling burns the hard, magical rock that will
begin to burn beneath the surface to become
bright glowing embers of radiating warmth, waiting
to replace the comfort of the heavy patchwork quilt.

Beth Turner Ayers
McKinney, Texas

Cortisol

I'm frightened of fire
I was in one working
At a hospital
Fought desires to leave

Thought I'd never see my
Daughter again
I moved post c-section women
Across the fire door

Hanging on to me
Were women gripping
As I was pushing wheelchairs
I cannot forget this

The women and I were saved
And I have replaced my fire alarm
My daughter's much older now
But I am frightened

Wendy Baron
San Antonio, Texas

Flames Lapping

No, not of hell
nor the aftermath of an earthquake
nor will the building burn down.
We interlock in the middle
of your brother's 70s upholstered
living room
olive, pumpkin, and gold tones
hold each other up but remain separate
a little soiled at the piping.
Little ghosts with eyes
flames flutter evenly along floorboards
the pointed cap of a monk's
hood eagerly awaiting
the stove and its wall the only cool spot
to shuffle to—
if we hang on tight enough the blackened iron
will keep us cool.

Pretend that a minute is an hour
an hour a day
and a day a year.
Fire on fire you're burning up
before the fire began
covering your face with one hand
but not hidden -- it took an introduction
from two circles away
and from the beginning a rain of
unspoken magic
one leading the other
hand through a lack of oxygen.
And now the room
will engulf us.

Laurel Benjamin
El Cerrito, California

In Regards to It

Intense as a passion in one's eyes,
ember when the passion burns down
Destructive, incinerating all in its path
yet, clearing space for new growth
taking life to make life
Hot air emanates from it
scorched skin, singed hair smell of it
Smoke thick or wispy,
black or white
rises from it
Comforting in its warmth
frightful as it spreads unchecked
necessary sometimes
unwarranted others

The planet is being destroyed by it
our world is all consumed by it
and we…
we are feeding it,
fanning the flames
with our selfish ways

Chris Billings
Schertz, Texas

Bonfire

While the flames flicker in the cool night air,
people gather around to feel its warmth.
Wood and cardboard are piled slowly to keep the flames
lit.
The pit built with bricks keeps the fire from going
astray.
As the fire burns slowly,
ashes pop and fly over the burning flames.
The warmth from the fire sends the chill away.
A gentle wind blows through the dark skies while
the moon shines brightly up above the clouds.
The flames flicker in the wind and start to disappear
as the heat is no longer felt in the middle of the night.

Birdman 313
Houston, Texas

Savonarola's Bonfires of the Vanities

I had even persuaded Botticelli
To sacrifice a painting to the bright flames
That flared and crackled, consuming and hungry,
In the heart of Piazza Signoria.

Maidens donated jewelry, face paints, spices,
Young men, playing cards and *carnivale* masks,
Their books by Dante, Ovid, and Boccaccio.
Crowd and fire roared at each new depredation.

In the chill dark, the blaze became a censer,
And through its purifying smoke, sent prayers
Of repentance even across the Arno.
I know our Lord heard each and every one.

But when I tried to prove my acts were of God
By stepping into coals of another fire,
And He sent rain to spare me this act of faith,
Why did the mob read this as His disfavor?

Those whose tokens I had burned that winter night
Rejected me. God's fire flared and quelled within.
I confessed, recanted, and confessed once more,
Was hung from a beam in the same Piazza.

And only the grace of the Lord whom I served
Kept me from living till the fire reached my feet.
My ashes were scattered in the Arno, but
I did no less for God than he had for me.

Christine H. Boldt
Temple, Texas

Palo Duro Fire

Red clay-stone and white gypsum form ruffles
below yellow, gray and lavender mudstone.
Spanish skirts line canyon walls –
amphitheater backdrop.

Diamondback rattlers
wild turkey   mule deer
observe evening performances near
Prairie Dog Town Fork of the Brazos River.

Flag-bearing cowboys race horseback
along canyon's rim – preamble to performance.

Lightning splits a juniper tree.
Dancers garbed in flame colors spin –
fly through the air; fight fires on prairie stage
depict pioneer life.

Tall tales, knee-slapping humor –
history of land wars: ranchers, sodbusters, Indians.

Fiddlers play poignant melodies
accompany square dance numbers:
"Buffalo Gal," "Old Joe Clark."

The story ignites
the grandeur blazes
the play sizzles –
"Texas!"

Von S. Bourland
Happy, Texas

A Tanka and Two Haiku

singed hearts grieve
injured and dying people,
firefighters, koalas…
protecting environments
not a world priority

----

barren landscapes
the cacophony
of sorrow

----

in the ashes
a glint of light
gran's ring

Claire Vogel Camargo
Austin, Texas

Fire and Ice

What hidden secrets lay in your smoldering flame?
Do I dare come closer and feel your intense potent heat
Unconsciously seducing me
Inviting me closer
To me submerged by your all-consuming power?
I hear the echoes of the fresh wood slowly being
annihilated
Crackling below the full moon this cold winter
night.
I involuntarily shudder as I pull my hands towards you
Trying my best to keep warm in the frozen hell around
me.
I stare at the flame
Completely mesmerized
By its bright red radiant light that captivates.
Only you can survive and battle with this bitter cold
That shows no mercy towards a wearied and feeble
human.
Keep burning,
Never die
And take me with you!
Submerge me completely with your fascinating
bewitchment
And prevail against this frozen inferno.
For only you can save me
As I long to be one with you
And unite forever in your everlasting flare.

Vanessa Caraveo
Los Fresnos, Texas

Take Fire, an Ozark Sonnet

Take wet February. Take the weeks after.
Take brush in the fields they clear with fire,
those farmers who swear its safe to burn,
who once were daredevil Ozark boys,
scanning hay fields for leaves in flame.
Boys in Black Cat bandoleers, holding their palms
to the blaze til they blister, boys who never
could put out their fever. Like them,
we were young. We believed in burning.
Cigarette butts sailed smooth out car windows.
When we were young we had nothing to lose,
up here where not much takes hold and grows.
It's pretty safe, is what farmers say,
where a scorched hillside can smoke for days.

Wendy Taylor Carlisle
Eureka Springs, Arkansas

Consumed

The first time I saw you,
I could not help myself.
The smile on your face,
The look of those bright eyes,
And the features you had
Made for passion spreading,
Like a wildfire
Raging out of control.

It was an inferno
That could never be stopped,
At least in my wild,
If not uncontrolled mind,
Lost in smitten feelings.

Yes, I had been consumed
With burning desire.
It was then that I knew,
Or so I thought I knew,
You were the one for me,
For now, and forever,
And forever after.

But then reality
Floored me like a car wreck,
And my world was not
The same for a long time.

A.J. Chilson
Princeton, Texas

Burn Off

Driving home late at night
Beacons appear on the horizon.
Sometimes you can even smell it,
The burn off happening late at night

Paeans to industry, let us now
raise our voices in exultations,
sing to petroleum, Babel recreated,
uniting us under the flag of petroleum
and fossil fuel dependence.

Holy fire burning away the
poverty in small, dirt road towns,
bathing men in crude and sweat,
rewarding them with wealth
everlasting and a truck in the driveway.

Let that fire long guide us home,
let the methane ever bear us
towards the holy factories,
pumping oil through our veins.

Karen Cline-Tardiff
Rockport, Texas

birth of the phoenix

not all flames are destructive,
i rose from the ashes
of the chaos you had given me
with the wings of a phoenix;
raven transformed into a mythical
and immortal daughter of the
moon
burning with every flaming tongue
of the sun star—
your falls and destructions don't define you,
every time you rise you prove you are
stronger than every scar etched
against your heart and skin;
these fires in my heart
will light the way to my success and my dreams—
it will lead me away from the darkness of you.

Linda M. Crate
Meadville, Pennsylvania

YOSEMITE - 1964

*Everyone needs beauty as well as bread, places to play
in and pray in, where nature may heal and give
strength to body and soul alike.*   John Muir

I remember Yosemite
when we all camped by the river in the valley
Row upon row of Volkswagen buses
People from all over the world
Lacquer boxes of sushi from Japan
Open face sandwiches, in wooden boxes from Denmark
Fried chicken and potato salad from Texas
Truly a place to play in and pray in.

Awe and wonder as fire
tumbled down Glacier Point just after sunset
Fire, so central to religious experience
in ancient cultures
There we sat under the stars, listening to the
hushed sounds of awe in a dozen languages
The deep silence that followed
We were not afraid, mystery held us close in that
sacred bowl of mountains and towering pines
Beauty brought us healing
In the universal language of nature
For one brief, spectacular moment —we were one.

Janelle Curlin-Taylor
Austin, Texas

Sacred Fire

Within this space is a fire,
burning and churning upward through
the middle channel of this meridian,
and I'm a coward,
hyped above previous expectations.
Shiva approaches
this feeble form of a somewhat
Romanesque style,
drawing me down to nothing,
from where being observes
to where being is I.

Christopher Danysh
San Marcos, Texas

Pompeii's Lover

You lay in all your splendor,
haughty in your grace, your beauty,
as if saying to Rome:
"You cannot hold a candle to me!
My buildings gleaming in white,
blind the eyes,
and are soothed by my cool blue bay.
You trudge on your seven hills,
panting like the she-wolf that whelped you."

In the distance, a brooding mount,
awaken by proud bruiting,
smolders with longing.
His blood bubbles from deep beneath,
rising at the sight of alabaster beauty.
There is no romance, no loveplay.
Vesuvius erupts, flooding her with his molten love,
taking her, in firey embrace.

And Rome, her callused feet slapping the hard stone,
wipes the sweat from a tanned brow,
and smiles.

Charles Darnell
San Antonio, Texas

A City Turning Its Back

Everyone understands
this wasn't an accident.

We watched the afternoons arrive carved up
staunching a wound
with just enough indifference.

Streets abandoned
while a city makes the most of losing.

We watch now
from the other shore

your flames say everything.

Judy DeCroce
Brockport, New York

Fire Purifies

You were created to make things hot
Most valuable when placed under pressure
The red desire of a burning flame
Wish you were here to melt away the pain

Just thinking about you makes me sweat
I need you to remove the things that don't belong
Make me clean with passionate warmth
Can't imagine not being in the fire with you.

My heart is aflame
The heat from your heart changes the shape of my
desire
Its shine brighter than gold.
Your love created something so beautiful

With you I feel no cold
Only a warmth from deep within.
Make me clean with your passionate flame
And purify me with fire.

Lula Ellis
North Richland Hills, Texas

A Spark That Became an Eternal Fire

Across a room I see the glow of a beautiful blaze
that captivated my eyes and feelings as I gazed.
Not understanding why I'm lured to this flame
causing warmth in my heart that won't soon wane.

I'm nearing a charming sparkle that's entrancing.
Will it stay burning, I wonder while glancing?
Is there fuel to buff it up and keep it simmering?
Seemingly attracted to me; do I see it lingering?

I move closer excited with each step taken.
The nearer I get; I become more awakened.
It's unclear why this encounter caused a spark,
surely not because the room was a little dark.

My infatuation with this radiance grows brighter.
As years go by, my affection is deeper and wider.
It remains an essential part of who I am today,
sharing an eternal love that will never fade away.

Decades have passed, the passion is still burning;
forever one, tied together by an early yearning.
Two hearts in unity now waiting for our last call,
never forgetting the small fire that started it all.

Manuel L. English, PhD
Poulsbo, Washington

Remember September, 2011?

We watch in dismay
as the flames lick the acres
quite clean on ranch lands all around us.

With a snap-crackle-pop,
cedar trees fuel the flames.
Relentless undoings astound us.

It's chilling to watch
how the heat of such fire
melts down those who try to defeat it.

Vast acres succumb.
Blackened land and thick smoke
taunt us all, 'til we boast "We beat it!"

By grace now, we know
what it means when they say
that "a miss is as good as a mile!"

Soon after the fires,
we were so gently told
"Propane tank has been leaking a while."

Nancy Fierstien
Dripping Springs, Texas

Ode to the Fire

You are beautiful and terrible.
We give you names:
Horseshoe, Aspen, Bighorn.
No matter how humble
or majestic, you follow
your own rules,
listen to the wind,
rage this way and then that.
Or fight for your life
against Hot Shot Firefighters
and planes that drown you
in chemicals and water.
Helicopters buzz you,
irritations like the real bees
that languish now
near burned out juniper.

As night approaches
your winking lights
ease on slowly
like your sister city down below
till the mountainside awakens,
then erupts, radiant
in her headdress
trimmed in brilliant gold.

Janice S. Fuller
Webster, Wisconsin

breaking through

between sitar and the rain annie's flute
paints flowers that will one day
explode through dirt and set the world on fire
not that there were any sitars playing
when maria came in drenched
          from walking   to the bus stop
            to the train
                to the school
I blush   ashamed at what it took
for me to see the flames of motivation
the golden flower it was my honor
to teach? pompous word for meager efforts
as if anything I do could quench her fire
could prevent her from breaking through
I hope a flute is playing when she finally
looks in the mirror and sees
that magnificent sunflower sees fields aflame
with wild flowers— sisters and brothers
blooming burning blooming
blooming everywhere

Alan Gann
Dallas, Texas

Hindu Kush

Vishnu in the Eternal City
getting carried away like a fresco
Barbarians have breached the Spanish Steps
priest & hobo warming hands by the fire
& the whores have been smoking all night
The Pride of Florence is arching her way upstairs
and like a cobra, you're charmed
better mutter a prayer, because in the morning
There will only be Krishna leaving your doorway

Christian Garduno
Ingleside, Texas

Here It Comes Again

There is no warning
this feeling of no purpose
downward trend of uselessness
the fire is gone, life is gone out of me.

The fire is gone again
gloom sets in once more
the very soul of worthlessness.
Pain burns deep within.

"Sacrifice for me!" is their mentality!
There is no reason for my living
except to die for the economy.

The fire is gone again; here it comes
that feeling of cold in my grave.
Society wants my blood
without a ventilator.

Tears dampen my aging skin
as I set in my home alone
with no fire left.

Barbara Terrell Goerdel
Arlington, Texas

Death of a Solipsist

One night, dreaming, I'm back in Seoul
in my apartment on the seventeenth floor.
Every light is off; I'm insomniac. My naked
body standing before a sliding glass window.

This night the city spills into the unlit room.
My image in the glass stares back at me,
also naked, and through him the parallel
streets and skyscrapers carve the city.

I can stand here for a small eternity.
For the first time I can see right through
myself, the straight lines and right angles
of moving headlights carving me up.

This time every night, the street vendors
are packing up, their bodies flashing
beneath electric billboards. Everyone
illuminated in the cities' great light.

The myth of us and them never existed
except in murderous imaginations.
Every where I've been -- burning in me,
and my afterimage burned into everything.

 D.A. Gray
Copperas Cove, Texas

Fire House

Abandoning the burning house, grab what you can.
Some clothes, a doll, letters, a laptop.
But what about the late night sex, the kitchen
lit by morning, coffee boiling, stew simmering,
and the couch, soft as a hundred arms.
Laughs, not likely. Love, we can only hope.
And looking back, what do we have?
A house with no roof, no glass.
A house without summer, without language,
without birth, without the Rolling Stones.
It's a fortress for ash to bear up against
old newspaper, tossed beer-can.
A toothless old man will crawl into
the shadow of its remaining wall,
He'll have a flea-ridden dog
that sleeps by his side.
But we'll do the scratching,
we'll do the yelping.

John Grey
Johnston, Rhode Island

Through The Fire

There's a forest fire raging inside me.
A chemical reaction that gives off light and heat.
A process of instance chemical combustion
And my soul has been set ablaze

Whenever she is near.
The hardest parts of me slowly melt away
A love is forged in an emotional furnace
She ignites the man inside of me.

Hot sketches sasche in my mind
While "sinnamom" incense smolders
Her smoke, evokes passions clearly undefined
ebony skin blushes with love's warm yearning

Together we are aflame
A burning mass of emotion
A brightly glowing display of pure romance
And I would go through the fire for her.

Michael Guinn
Irving, Texas

Uriel's Visitation

The builder knows what he has built can't last
forever, but to watch it burn before his eyes
singes his soul, never to recover.

The house, built with his hands, designed
with shelves just the right height for her,
with two sinks and rooms for grandkids,
a place to know who you are,
where you come from - gone.

Men and boys in yesterday's barn listening
to the engine of the restored tractor turn over,
purr like grandma's cats - gone.

All the labor, all the pleasure, all the purpose
of this place consumed to ash —
a bird feeder, charred, standing alone,
relic to some apocalyptic sword
slicing the flesh of Christ,
eviscerating the blessed community
trying to stand on its knees —
an unquenchable prophecy.

Ken Hada
Ada, Oklahoma

Like a Low Sweet Flute

Like a low sweet flute
The dove calls from the warm oak at midday;
The geraniums gather sunlight,
Their red petals reminding us
Of the lava, fire colored,
In secret volcano crevices.

In each of us there are reeds
Waiting for the summer wind
To make music.
There is a flower,
Powered by fire,
Waiting to bloom.

Rose Anna Higashi
Ka'a'wa, Hawaii

Flashpoint

This combustible society
is ablaze
like cottonwood kapok
soaked in kerosene
and lit
with a flamethrower.
O, that a rain
of common sense
might douse
the incendiary
rhetoric!
Let a flood
of peaceful rationality
turn the rising tide
of chaos,
that it may ebb
and flow back
from whence it came!
We are better than this.

Camille Hill
Deming, Washington

Fire Tender

The diseased hand sleeps in a glove
Leather protects and provided stability

Thirty years the joints have burned
Fueled by excessive movement
Like the burning bush of Moses
The fire continues and is not consumed

Thousands of pills have not
Extinguished the flames
Fiery pulsations interrupt
Middle of the night slumber

Tending the fire is fatiguing
It is a life-long task

Sandi Horton
Woodway, Texas

Prometheus in a Scottish Pub

North Sea blusters within spitting distance.
Wind from Scandinavia, muscular and damp,
drives flecks of ice like steel needles.
We've come to view cathedral ruins from 1158,
just one long putt beyond St. Andrew's ninth hole.
Somewhere between Butt Wynd and tour bus,
leaden feet and bone chill blunder us
into a little pub where, disregarding UK history
as we Yanks are wont to do, we order Irish coffee.
The friendly barman agrees to fetch coffee
owt tha nebraw, laces it liberally with Jamison's.

Joanne, like a young Elizabeth Taylor,
flashes him her ten-thousand-watt smile
and over tips, which inevitably
reduces barmen and waiters to devoted servitude.
Our tall glass cups empty quickly,
and Joanne orders another round.
Warmth traces slow spirals through chests
till faces glow. We've seen enough ruins today,
raise our cups; the gods have gifted us with fire.

Ann Howells
Carrollton, Texas

Stew

Cast iron pan and flame embrace,
embryonic shapes marinate.

Spicy flavors infuse the group
in a brewing alphabet soup.

A ladle dips a gumbo bowl,
salt and pepper imbue the whole.

Zesty noodles twist in the mix.
Infinity's breath blows hot sips.

Served up in evolution's dome,
all hope, and a simmering moan.

Lisa Hubley-King
Dripping Springs, Texas

The Pensacola Fireman
A Terza Rima

A Florida firefighter has shown little fear,
with enthusiasm that never seemed to stop.
He was awarded "firefighter of the year,"

A firefighter is different than a cop,
fighting fires can be quite a chore.
but his performance is up at the top.

He saved a woman's life on the fifth floor,
a woman was wedged between a wall and a bed.
They carried her down the stairs to level four.

He saved her life; she could've been dead,
but waiting for workers he gave her first aid.
The firefighters award didn't get to his head.

His loyalty to his company he never betrayed,
humility for a brave man who isn't afraid.

Mark Hudson
Evanston, Illinois

Salamander

Salamander dances on the cauldron's edge
reveling in flame, singing along in her cracked voice
to the uneven rhythm of popping cinders and crackling
branches.
The longest day has barely passed and twilight lingers
in the hills.
Impatient Luna makes her early entrance with dainty
Venus at her side
trailing glory clouds flushed pink and rosy as recently
kissed lips.
It's party time, a sister celebration; wine, women, fruit
and song
to honor the One Who Honors Life with Love, she who
comes humbly
to the Lion Throne but knows how to roar like a
warrior. Courage
is her watchword and She is faithful to her word.
Look how women dance around her, beating drums,
yip-yip-yipping at the sky. A new year is birthing,
may it be rich with blessing; fruitful and abundant
Aho, sings the salamander
Aho, chorus the frogs
Aho, echo the hills
So say we all.

Christine Irving
Denton, Texas

Before They Say Goodnight

Evening, the weight of my world set down for the night.
A seat at the backyard fire pit, flames dancing circles
around the surface of a blue glass pond.

Overhead a few stars. I remember the night
we went to the observatory and saw the embers
of a dying star a thousand or more light years away.

A star whose flame was extinguished by the time
we could see its faint glow through the telescope.
Sometimes I look into the constellations of your eyes

and see an entire universe with my heart,
and I wonder how many light years have these stars
already traveled to reach me before they say goodnight.

Mark Jodon
Houston, Texas

The Night the Fire In My Dad's Heart Died

My nightly adolescent chore
Tending the den fireplace
Mother stared while Father snored.
I watched the flames trace
Shadows on the black back bricks
Inside our home's hearth
Soot built up so thick
Like the arteries in my Father's heart.
He awoke in his favorite chair
I poked the logs with care
He uttered a low pained groan
Mom left for bed-I felt so alone
"Do you mind if I stay here with you" he sighed
"Of course not. I love you" I replied
"I know. Well, I'm really tired"
He creaked to his room. Entranced by the fire
I cried as I watched the embers expire...

Ken Jones
Gonzales, Texas

Fire Fight

You asked for a poem
regarding fire
and I was fired up to write one
but I could not think of
fire without hell
a hell of a note to be sure
yet fire became an obsession
I played with matches
I poured gasoline on words
hoping an idea would start
but still nothing would ignite
so my flame became
a burnt wick
blackened as a fish
no spark
no flame
no poem
the fire never started
but still there is that desire
a fire that burns within
to write a poem
about fire.

David Knape
Rowlett, Texas

When Teen Under Quarantine Has Had Enough

The slam of the door when you storm out
burns into me. The flame you leave behind
is met with fear, my thoughts return to doubt.
The slam of back door when you storm out
urges me to think about the summer drought
singing thin skin. House arrest my mind
slammed like the door when you stormed out.
Burn into me, the flame you leave behind.

Laurie Kolp
Conroe, Texas

When the Sun Appears

Napa Valley winds swirled
around bone-dry hills swelled
to fires refueled themselves
leapt roads both sides of the valley
drove smoke and flames her way.
I walked paths into carpet
waited for texts, watched news --
smoke muffled morning
in bloodshot haze, veiled vineyards
and streets of lone chimneys
rose stunned among toothpick trees.
At last her call came through tears of relief.
But flames kindled downtown
as she worked in gas mask
to photograph vineyards still standing
brought extras to field hands
rested her lungs at night.
I longed to beg her to come home.
She will visit but her work is there
for when the smolder clears
for when the sun appears.

Mary Anna Scenga Kruch
Williamston, Michigan

At the Cabin

Heavy rain, a constant companion,
showed no sign of stopping
as we drove toward our lodgings
on the first leg of our road trip.

A small rustic log cabin,
doorway pooled with water,
few amenities and bare fireplace
greeted our weary eyes.
Cold and damp inside,
I longed to build a fire,
to pull the only chair,
a rocker, in front of the fireplace,
watch flames lick wood,
hear the snap, crackle, and pop
as wood was devoured,
reduced to embers that glowed,
cast shadows on bare walls
like it had at my grandparents'.

There was no wood to be had,
no matter how much I wanted it.
Sadly, I finally went to bed,
wrapped in memories of fires
that had warmed long-ago.

Catherine L'Herisson
Garland, Texas

From Whence They Came

The words are for no eyes
but my own.
Burned onto the page,
pen moving with a mind of its own,
Angry thoughts and words
scrawl hard and dark,
Embossing one page
deeply into the next.
Thoughts honored as valid and important,
my mind breathes a sigh of relief.
These words and thoughts are mine alone
and do not deserve to see the light of day...
Should never reach anyone's ears or
scorch a dear heart.
They blast from the fires of hell,
carrying certain destruction in their claws.
Mind sated, paper saturated,
here is this dark dross of no consequence.
I carry the angry words to a patch of
dry, parched ground and strike a match.
Fire curls the edges and burns bright,
taking the hot words and thoughts…
Back to the inferno from whence they came.

Susan Mardele
McKinney, Texas

flame of life

is it possible to inflame, excite,
set the heart aflutter
does a heart burn out
from intense or passionate fire?
does the love come freely
as heartbeats to child from mother?
or can love spark off from someone other?
what spirit powers a torch
to kindle an ardent flame?
does passion come from the heart
or from the brain?
when hot arrows in flames sent flying pierce
it is in the chest that our spirit stirs
and bursts fierce
oh let that passion once more actuate
to urge me
send life-giving blood to replenish
and surge through free
for once the fire flickers and smolders out
it has done it's work
and leaves fuel for new life to sprout

Jack McCabe *nom de plume magicjackatx*
Austin, Texas

Fire and Ice

We're celebrating Emily's birthday
in a Conroe bar. She is 189 years old
today. The big café dark, a few dim
lamps here and there, and we are reading
our poems with hers. Waiting our turn
and listening, we sit on chairs, boxes, stools.
I sit on the stone hearth next to the fire.
It's chilly so I lean toward it, but lo,
it's a fake fire! Logs spark, flames lick upward,
but no heat! I slip my hand behind
the screen and touch a log. Nothing.
I can't reach the flames but the whole
display is just slightly warm to touch
like a computer. My name called,
I set my iced tea by the grate, step up
to read, the fire winking in the back.
When I get back, the firelight
catches the ice, shimmers, glitters.
I wonder could we stop the world
from ending, using only fire and ice?
They look beautiful together, like friends,
the fake firelight shining in the cubes.

Janet McCann
College Station, Texas

A Fire On The Prairie

At first, danger is only a subtle scent.
A doe lifts her head from grazing.
Two squirrels pause from chatter.

The wind brings a raw smell of smoke.
The western sky darkens. Soon, fire
appears, a half-mile wide. Creatures
panic, flee before it. Many perish.

Cows escape by plunging into a pond.
Their bawling can be heard for miles.
Wild horses gallop, reach safety in the hills.

Several barns are lost before courageous
firefighters subdue the demon.
One day later only char remains.

A year from now the land will green.
Butterflies will dance to the plaintive notes
of a meadowlark; cattle will graze once more,
proving that the prairie lives forever.

LaVern Spencer McCarthy
Blair, Oklahoma

What Is It About a Fire?

Dutiful as woodsmen
we stack our days
like firewood
some saved
some split
some too rotten
to burn
then one afternoon
when we feel a chill
we lay one memory
atop another within
the circle of stones
we call our past
and given
the crackle and spit
the rage and roar
the insistence
of carbon greedy for heat
we set our world ablaze
in a rowdy combustion
a staggering conflagration
whose ashen breath joins
the cloud of regrets
that we exhale
into the fiery glow
of time being consumed
like fuel for a fire
as we stare blankly
into sparks of light
wondering where
the years have gone

Anne McCrady
Tyler, Texas

Brushfire Revolt

Brushfire across the country.

Revolt throughout the Arab world.
Abused land is irritated.
People are burning inside,
Hungering for something better
Than what the slick waiter has served.

The high winds of disgust have spread
The uprising and assisted
Every blade of grass to sparkle
And form one self-immolation.
Blazing uncontained flames caught on,
Shutting down store and fields of work.

Acres charred and palaces toppled.
Irate weeds so parched they had scorched
Through the landowner's tall fences.

I fan myself, but the heat is different here.
They say, discomfort does not affect everyone.

Joshua Meander
Woodside, New York

Virtual Dinner

First, I smelled something malodorous
seeping through my air vent.
Then, I heard a repetitive high pitch noise-
zing, zing, zing something akin to the sound
of a fire truck, coming from the main house.
Aghast, from the kitchen *fire* alarm system!

With quickened steps, heartbeats racing,
I reached the kitchen, and there she was,
my granddaughter, frantically working on
stopping the *fire* alarm system as meat
on the overheated frying pan started to burn,
meat fat sparking up and down igniting *fire*.

Finally, the alarm ceased, but not the teardrops
that sneaked out from her large brown eyes.
The now blackened meat did not look like a bit
as shown in the picture of the recipe she,
and her friend from a faraway U.S. State
agreed to cook for their first dinner together.

Resurgence of Coronavirus deprived him of
seeing her face-to-face, in lieu, him, and my
granddaughter agreed to have a virtual dinner—
from planning the meal, to cooking at the same
time, to setting the table, and to dining together.
Alas, budding love put off by the frying pan *fire*!

Sylvia S. Medel
McKinney, Texas

Ball of Fire

Thunder shook our windows. Wind
moved the barn two inches, and then
there was the ball of fire big
as a tractor tire that
came rolling through
the living room
into the kitchen
struck the frig
dissolved and
knocked out the electricity.

We sat stunned huddled
on the couch, staring
at the fire ball's path
wondering
what if one of us had

been standing in
the middle of the room
walked to the frig
or doubted the
supremacy of nature.

Marianne Mersereau
Lake Forest Park, Washington

Maternal Fire

To my dear daughter Victoria,

I can not give you an answer
for Eve or her apple, nor can I
unravel roles without a discomfort.
I can tell you, the cord
linking between us remains, and

maturing feels like butterfly in reverse.
But there can be heaven in moments
of attribute, a softness, to sing
the endearment of matriarch.
History has led us into fire.

There is blood
in our ancestry, yes, but fire
still rises on the horizon.
A blaze more collective than we.
As kindness is not weakness,

and roots of mother trees
have been known to lift foundations.
I can tell you… the beginning
is never like the end at all.

Nicole M. Metts
Copperas Cove, Texas

"a conflagration"

feel it in the throat, a flare
maybe not rage, but what should be said
sparked by a word or two or three
building, it hurts.
a choice:
breathe out, and flames burst from lips.
"fire breather," "aggressor," "witch."
or swallow, stifle the flames;
metamorph into coal and sit in the stomach, a weight
stays unsaid, invokes nothing.
but other words stoke,
pharynx inflames, no longer a decision
the truth a conflagration, eyebrows singed.

Leslie Michaels
Waco, Texas

Burned

Our affair began with sparks,
a smattering of stars.
But when they ignited,
the flames swelled into the sky
and embarrassed the sun.
We burned, entwined, not minding
if it triggered our destruction.
But the flames consumed our limbs.
Inexorably, we faded, shrunk,
became unrecognizable.

This was the only way that it could end.

Watching, I feel the heat, a blanket.
I hear the crackle as the walls fry.
My eyes are dry.
A shelter shape-shifts to a furnace.

I imagine his face
as he sees what I've undone.
Sirens slice the darkness,
but I will not run.
I'll complete our cremation
before, like smoke, I rise.

Jen Mierisch
Lincolnwood, Illinois

The Night the Moon Caught Fire

When we stepped into the garden
wind parted the tree branches—

above us clouds appeared
like puffs of smoke

as if the moon was on fire
and only we could see

the sun's jealous face
as dawn pretended to sleep.

Michael Minassian
Flower Mound, Texas

Roadside Crowns

Traveling a mountain highway in search of an uncommon
path.....one leading
to virgin grasses nestled between verdant bosoms, vibrant
with twinkling aspens, a jubilee of life soaking up
clear snow waters, sharing joy with purple wildflowers

Anxiously I yearned to wrap my weary bones around white
barked magnificence, in homage to primitive palisades of
my
Appalachian birth....so long ago

The ache in my heart became a fire in my belly with each
sighting of homemade wooden crosses stuck
in dry earth, wearing faded flowers for a crown of thorns,
a reminder of a life once loved and perhaps now forgotten,
dreams ended

I have seen such crosses in my travels, never like this,
I passed one, two, three, then six, several groupings of five,
I lost count at thirty death enshrouded monuments
Flames engulfed my marrow with regret, my prayers cried
out
for a thurible of incense, for
a cleansing ..no.. a scrubbing of my dark spirit

I pulled my truck into an abandoned road, no longer gated,
the distant peaks became a goliath of
promise, a welcome home party of aspens,
mountain streams, sacredly anointing,
beckoning me with outstretched fire quenching hop

Zee Mink-Fuller
Crowley, Texas

Autumn fire

And when the Autumn sun splits asunder
Plunging me in the waves of heat
When the blue ahead blends in cinnabar
There the temple, sculpted browning,
aureoled in saffron robes
My brown skin turning golden
My marrow becoming crimsoned like the fallen leaves
Ravishing, reddish, Sandpaper-ish, sepia
I grasped in the breath song of the dusk
 as the Birds' singing in the winds
Brings a Mellow rhythmic tune
I sit with flames overpowering,
Blue blood orange enmeshed in my ribs
I hold the burning within my iris- pure
as from whcrc Draupadi arose.
The landscape like a land of Agni
Teeming, hot, ablaze
As I watch the fiery sheen around
sit yearning, waiting for you-
Until the first showers monsoonal,
Soothe and douse the pain aglow.

S. Rupsha Mitra
Kolkata, West Bengal, India

Diminish

My cells remember the light of an old me,
who danced to calling seas.
The beauty of their ringing lament
struck the flint of youth in her muscles.
Her movements were worship, singing,
"I am here!"
Then whispers like smoke crept inside her to say,
"Enough—too much—too much of you."
They turned to nicotine and
"too much, too much" was not enough.
The sea became a tuning fork;
a hurricane held to her ear.
She put out dancing like a cigarette,
and smaller,
smaller,
she grew to be less—
leftover ash that remembers the heat,
and cells that remember the light.

Kayla Mize
Waco, Texas

Fire Flies at the Balloon Fiesta

Balloons prepare for ascension as
October dawn awakens over Albuquerque
Where aeronauts are reimagining first flight

Prisms of color in shapes of
Inverted water droplets and so many more
Gently lie pronate near their wicker baskets
Bestrewn across open pastures

Crews begin to slowly inflate giant
Envelopes of fabric with fans until
Air billows within awaiting transformation

Burners are lit creating
Sounds of giant blowtorches
Echoes of ancient magma exploding from earth

Like Athena breathed life into man
Fire breathes hot air into the balloons
Creating buoyancy
Giving lift
Commanding flight
To once lifeless forms

Susan Munsch
Houston, Texas

May Fire

Fire around the stone circle casts leaping light
On sarsen stones — on naked skin.

Words flicker lambent flames inside
Replenishment, fulfill, furrow and reap.

Blazing arcs through night firmament Pleiades
Intensifies burning passion crackling flame.

Wind carried sweet hawthorn's pungent reek
Earshot men's voices chant across the causeway.

"Snake. Woman. Moon." "Hear those beasts
Calling for your womb? Ride their plows to reap."

Riotous naked women and men ignite the bonfire.
Snake Goddess' burning fields' desire combusts.

Tom Murphy
Corpus Christi, Texas

I Am Drama Darlin'

Oh Darlin',
before you seek sweet comfort from my dewy lips,
Yet truly, I am an unruly dragon dressed in drag.

Oh Darlin',
my will flows through my veins like molten steel.
I shall not be trifled with. Gaze into my eyes.
See two cauldrons percolating liquid fire. Then,
run your hand down my feather soft body. Feel
scaly armor beneath sinewy muscles capable of
pulverizing little ol' you. Feel my talons rake
your delicious flesh while you stroke my back.
Touch pleated wings ready to fly me away,
leaving you lonely. A burnt shell of yourself.

Oh Darlin',
your besotted self would miss my hot danger.
I am untamed fire. I am drama Darlin'!
A dragon in drag who can be yours…if you dare.

Ann Marie Newman
Richardson, Texas

It's called... fire!

Far from a friend it is....
It knows no borders
It keeps no lovers
It burns centres...
And razes quarters
It's called...
Fire!
Inferno is its name...
It needs no fame
For it is a flame...
None can tame...
Neither by claim
Nor by shame
It's called...
Fire!
Requires no invitation...
Yet comes on obligation...
To cause trouble in a nation...
And let dire ramification...
The mother of perdition
It's called...
Fire!
Everyone must learn...
To defend its clan
From this stern...
That knows none,
And has no fun
It's called...
Fire!

Otieno Lawi Ondiek
Kisumu, Kenya

Almost Unnoticed

Like the good neighbor she is she calls
Confessing this will take longer than expected
She will call sometime tomorrow
Today is boring, ordinary as usual.

Quiet small mountain communities
People mind their own business
Sawmill up the mountain runs
In regular order slicing logs to lumber.

Admiring the peaceful view
Almost unnoticed in the distance
Dark smoke streaks the sky
Uninvolved fellow citizens become involved.

Echoes of warning screech across the land
Suddenly flames flicker and crackle
A few brave souls rush to the danger
Others ready to protect their lives, property.

Indiscriminate, tongues of fire rage
Destroy property, labor, loves, lives
Dreams, plans, hopes instantly disappear
Leaving ashes, bent metal, hollow promises.

Like political life in 2020
Destruction comes unannounced
But the effects last forever.

Michael Owens
Cypress, Texas

Ravaged

At five my world collapsed in bombs
that took my parents' precious home
one frightful night.
Next day we left
in borrowed clothes.
The house had burned into a shell
and only one small flame still licked
the attic way up high,
past living room and bedroom floors
and our Opa's attic suite.
No toys or books,
no clothes or food
survived the bombs.
Our shell-shocked lives
were burned-out empty like the house.
And if we dared to cling to things
from that day on, my mother said:
enjoy possessions while you can,
but don't get married to a thing.

Christa Pandey
Austin, Texas

A Comfy Chair

Not ready for a warm blanket and a comfy chair
 in front of the fire, to satisfy my basic needs.
While actually living in the now, I still maintain
my many pivotal-memories of what was.

My Earth life has never been particularly easy.
I've often felt, I'm walking through quicksand,
or hot-coals to prove something to someone.
My body, cumbersome feet, paid the burden.

Undergoing my internal, Self-Imposed drama,
I've found myself exhausted, isolated and worried.
Not what expected, but emotions push me through.
Glaring, pummeling-issues for change always there.

A great idea, not merely a sugar-coated pretense.
I'm ready for the glorious, celebratory-fireworks.
I changed issues with my role, which excites me.
And totally accomplished my major success steps.

Hearth firelights of home welcome me to party.
No more fear, or drama, as the sky is Not falling.
In truth, it's simply changing, as a fire-sun sinks
off the horizon, becomes a peach-colored moon.

I allow myself to know my joy, my soul-role.
Not responsible for shifting others' quagmire.
I've skills to share and do Not stagnate in place.
More sunbeams, I ignite-sparks of transition.

Alice Parker
Prosper, Texas

Flame: A Zombie Zonnet

I remember when we were in high school
reeling in the heat of the first flame
the youth, the exhaustion, the passion
the intense yearning and raw tenderness
like innocent rabbits without regard
having our intimate way with ourselves

presently, beyond those amazing years
within the largest closest in the house
wearing the same chains our dog once wore
lunging at me every time she sees me
offering the freshest of meat to be found
as it becomes rarer each time I hunt

death seems forever, but I kept my part
sex, however, is now a bit awkward

Juan M. Perez
Corpus Christi, Texas

House Fire

Any firefighter will tell you,
it is the fire between the walls …
unseen and ignored
that is most dangerous.

Smoldering or fully ablaze
behind walls, the fire unnoticed
will eventually consume the house.
Any firefighter will tell you that.

putting out a raging grease fire in the kitchen
does not make the house safe.
One must look for, listen for, and feel for
the signs of … restrained heat … behind walls.

Even when compassionate and perceptive neighbors
rally to show support,
fires deferred and unheard
will incite if left unchecked, ignored behind walls.

Unacknowledged and discounted
this type of rage (excuse me) … fire
will burn a nation (excuse me) … house
down.

Any firefighter will tell you that.

DaRell Pittman
San Antonio, TX 78253

Fire Watcher

What is this thing fire,
That dares challenge the night
And is not consumed therein;
That beckons the eye
Like moths to bathe,
And speaks to my very soul?

Surely it lives—like a spirit lives—
Cleansing and taking away, without prejudice;
Dust to dust—
But what of giving?

Surely it gives—like a river gives—
When it has swept and washed away,
And green returns all the greener.

Like a woman dances in a man's mind,
It dances in the man's eyes;
In verses spoken and unspoken,
To his infinite ear—
It speaks and the man listens.

Off in the distance the fire awaits,
Like a pillow of comfort in the night,

And the man and the moth,
Strangely intertwined, come,
Captive of the flame.

Gerald Plant
Waco, Texas

Dark Night

Wanting change. Hoping for something different.
Praying for something better.
Here is the catch. The old has to stop.
Stop. Stop. Gone. Burned up.
The loud breath whooshed through the garage.
Gasoline fumes catch the tiny spark in the gas water
heater
And blow it across the porch through the attic into the
house.
Burned up our history. Not enough for each other.
Burned up our lives as we had known them.
Fire can do that.

Jiaan Powers
Dallas, Texas

A Prayer for These Pandemic Times

Lord, ignite a fire in me
for understanding different views,
for loving those not easy to love,
for weathering the unknown winds of this storm,

Lord, help me to rekindle the flames of hope
when embers of truth seem to be fading.

Lord, restore my passion for words
so the ones I write may spark
a loving desire in my readers.

For I know that when I keep my eyes
on the glowing light of Your love,
my spirit is regenerated
like a roaring campfire.

Betty Roberts
Denton, Texas

The Holocaust Of A Disease

Pandemic
unseen
unquenchable fire
from multiple barrels
shooting red-hot coals of destruction
ravaging cities, towns and communities

invisible crimson flames
reaching unknown heights to the sky
hideously defiling atmosphere

combusting hearts of men
women and children
igniting prisons of confusion
flaming a bewildering glow of
panic and fear

immobilizing future plans
hopes and dreams
disseminating them into
smoldering lava like ashes

This pestilence, a frightful
igneous blaze - perhaps, a judgment
for all the irreverence in this world
shunning the fire of the Diety's
raging splendor, of unending love.

Irene C. Robertson
Little Elm, Texas

Lifetime of Desire

Strange, new, forbidden,
intoxicating, dangerous, secret.
They said she was "playing with fire."
Discovering an ancient secret
for the first time.

Grabbing passion by the tail,
Avoiding the sting
of the scorpion.
Love and sex burning in her
like fine brandy.

Honoring, enjoying each other
and the long years
of hallowed strength,
deep embrace.
Taking time to stoke the flame.

Susan J. Rogers
Georgetown, Texas

Frederick's Fire

The Mother of Exiles is calling out a name…
Of a proud, brave, plantation-born slave
Who escaped his chains
Who wrote so powerfully, eloquently
For the abolition of slavery: Frederick Douglass!

Lady Liberty stands tall
Engulfed in the flames of American injustice
Frederick would know how to douse the flames
To finally heal the burns of horrible hypocrisy
To bring our nation together as one

The year Lady Liberty's cornerstone was laid
Fred Douglass spoke on Emancipation Day
Although great progress had been made
Freedom is just one spoke in the wheel of liberty
We must open our arms to one another

Lady Liberty shines her torch all over the world
Freedom, justice, the pursuit of happiness
Equality, compassion, human dignity
Extends to all people in the global village
Frederick would smile on those words

The Mother of Exiles is calling out names:
Your name and my name…
She knows the hour is at hand
She knows it's time for all of us to take a stand

Lady Liberty's torch shines with Frederick's fire!

Barry Rynk
McKinney, Texas

Revelation

I had no idea that I was destined to become
a fire walker,
stepping barefoot onto glowing,
hot coals
without allowing them to singe my soles
or my soul.
"The fire is cold," says the fire master,
and I steel my mind,
my Self, in preparation. Still,
hot…glowing…coals,
daring me, taunting me, "Are you
brave enough
to walk on the fire of your life
without getting burned
beyond recognition?" Or perhaps
that's the whole point
of this journey: transformation,
if you are willing
to become the phoenix.

The trick is to not burn your feet
even as the rest of you goes up in flames.

I am a fire walker.

Cindye Sablatura
Pearland, Texas

faith is the fire

faith is the fire that burns within,
the hope that keeps us moving forward,
igniting the imagination,
joy and creativity,
enkindling belief.

faith is the fire that burns within,
the light that guides,
warmth that keeps us alive.
determined, we don't give up;
this fire is too great
to be extinguished,
buoying the spirit.

faith is the fire that burns within,
catching on as we spread hope,
passing the torch,
sharing what keeps us going,
what we are passionate about,
and illuminating sparks of faith
in others,
brightening the sky,
stars aglow.

Kathryn Sadakierski
Westfield, Massachusetts

Fire for Change

In 1969, the Cuyahoga River caught fire.
It only burned for thirty minutes
but the event helped change America forever.
A symbol for needed advancement,
after the fire on the river, laws were passed,
a new agency created, Earth Day born.

Today, the Country has caught fire.
Not the flags, buildings, or churches,
but the hearts of the people for a new world.
Black or White, full of hate or full of love,
all see the need for a different way;
hearts afire must make a change or blaze.

Does the color of the first firebuilder matter?
Does it matter the first firebuilder's gender?
Does their birthplace or their religion matter?
Does it matter what evil or good that fire
has been servant of in the story of humanity?
You cannot reply "Let us forget how to burn."

Stephen Sanders
Fort Worth, Texas

I Had Set a Match

A list folded on itself—Once, twice.
A flame set to its edges—Here, there.
An angst consuming the words—Some, all.
A spark resurrected, ha!—Flares, runs.
The cycle repeating itself—Once, twice.
The ash lifeless at last—Small, dead.
An end slower than I'd hoped—But, still.
A match is what it'd taken—Just one.

I was naïve to think my progress
Would be quick and clean, for
In amazement and dismay I observed
The cleansing fire find fuel
In trauma hidden and patterns ingrained,
Embers flaring and snaking
Along their own strange paths.
And as for the list, it had writhed as it died,
Shrinking until it was unrecognizable,
Leaving a pile of messy ash behind.
But progress was made, and that because I tried.
Indeed the unlearning of everything that set me
Back was neither instant nor straight-forward,
But it was destined, for
I had set a match.

April Scheffler
Houston, Texas

Enchantment

Flames snake around one log
and crawl to another,
a serpentine signature,
sealing the fate
of everything placed before it.
Charred remains,
simmering embers
glow with menacing fangs.

We stare into the expanding chasm,
drawn into its lair
to seek comfort and enlightenment,
transformed by the imbroglio,
pacified by its enchanting dance.
We are enveloped
and rendered helpless
as it drives to consume.

Witness it overpowering
and searing every obstacle,
thriving in a wide swath.
Give it something to yearn for
and it will conquer it,
pure power extinguishing life.

Stephen Schwei
Houston, Texas

Mouth on Fire

A little packet
"Taco Sauce"
Not labeled mild
Not labeled hot
  Just "Taco Sauce"
Like a car with the radio
Turned up to the max
No music is heard
No melody or tones
Of well-played instruments
Just noise
A cacophony of sound
Not music
Eardrum assault.
The red substance
The "Taco Sauce"
Might be a song
A nice tasty melody
Or might be a
Discordance of flavors
With no obvious taste
Just heat, Scoville Units galore
Gums on fire, taste buds dead
Mouth assault
Heartburn imminent

Elaine Fields Smith
Dublin, Texas

Burning Shadow (Kathleen in '78)
  (*Only lost love lasts forever.* Anon.)

Whether I loved you or not,
you are the one I can't forget.
You, whose breath seemed flower sweet,
whose body smelt of chamomile
with hair like a flood of henna…

Your thin rose lips' cool kisses
launched me into a sea of fire
where each slender finger was a brand
as you arced over me like lightning
stunning the dark…

        Hush now, forever,
burning shadow!

Bradley R. Strahan
Woodway, Texas

Mischief on Jamaica Beach

Wind rose in the night and blew the autumn
moon away. In darkness, the kids next door
played with fire. Its sparks like flaming arrows.
We worried the blaze from inside until
it shrank to embers. In the morning,
heavy drops cut through the ashes
while hearty gusts lifted sea spume like a kite
and flung it across the dunes to the panes
of our French doors. Then the wind partnered
with the chairs on the porch, sent them flying
down the stairs like expectant lovers.
We rushed out to pull them from outstretched arms
like parents saving daughters from the likes
of James Dean. Jilted, the wind pirouetted
and grabbed the flickering candle
on my writing desk. Tongues of fire skittered
over my poems, new partners for a mating dance.
I cried out at the flame's unexpected kiss.
A damp towel, a slammed door,
stamped out the fire's kindling passion
for words. The wind still looking for trouble.

Sandi Stromberg
Houston, Texas

Raku

Those in recovery, not just dry,
but sober, are baptized in fire.
Like fired pots, the results
are not uniform, carry the beauty
of imperfection. They have
stepped off their pedestals,
placed their feet on solid ground,
no longer driven, released
into humble compassion, survived
the fire, glad to be standing
in the scent of smoke.

Jeffrey L. Taylor
Austin, Texas

Sonnet to St. Valentine, Martyr, Buried on the
Flaminian Gate

Oh, if we could love the way swans love –
every feather white with holy promise.
Or the chimney's brickish embrace
of the aftermath of fire –
how it lifts to the stars.

Is there a Greek myth about
someone trying to kill love?
Does the moon resent
getting roped into love?

Notice how morning fog descends first
on the most vulnerable reach of the firs.
Think of the hawk watching her mate
leave the nest, crossing the distance
with a predator's hunger.

Colette Tennant
Salem, Oregon

The Winter Porch

Slivered newsprint shivers,
catches evening's embers
twinkling in the *chimenea.*
Kindling takes hold, emboldens the blaze,
burns peppery *pinon* with a comfortable crackle.
Orange serpentine flames
strike the crumpled paper,
toast the marshmallow
to a sweet, blackened crisp.

Smoky red wine mulls the day's recall -
listening to the Native American flute,
silvery notes played by men whose hearts can cry
at the music's prayerful plea -
and the deer,
warm brown, running, leaping
along wooded Highway 31
toward a sunset drink
in the nearby Neches River.

Glowing embers ignite,
fly, fill the air
like Methodist liturgy on Communion Sunday.

Carol Thompson
Tyler, Texas

Granny's Mojo

Granny knew where the slots were
She balanced on her wooden cane
and filled her lungs with good luck

She crouched like a tiger,
picking up the scent, the cosmic aura
of a slot-machine she preferred

I watched her eyes change colors—
from red to yellow to green
as the rows of fruit spun and changed

"Set the night on fire," she said
in a voice that could turn a lion
into a lamb

She touched the face of the machine,
making its lights flash with approval,
and numbers rotating on the screen

"No time to wallow in the mire," she sang
"We can only win more money
Come on, baby, take me higher!"

The vouchers came pouring out
of the one-armed bandit's mouth,
it began to rock, smoke, and catch fire

As the casino staff doused the flames,
Granny stuffed the vouchers in her purse
and let everyone know her mojo's back again.

Mark Tulin
Santa Barbara, California

Summer Night Salvation

We circle the glowing campfire,
Seeking solace and precious peace.
Flames leap like ballerinas,
We are mesmerized by the dance.

We speak in hushed tones,
Making way for the night sounds
Of cricket, owl, and frog.
They soothe our soul with their song.

They muffle the clamor of anger,
They quell the flames of hate,
They cover the night with a balm,
Healing our hearts with each verse.

The fire wraps us in its smoky arms,
Tensions and worries unwind, unwind.
We melt like marshmallows into our canvas chairs,
And drift into dreams of a different tomorrow.

Karen Vail
Flemington, New Jersey

Drapes too*

Fire out equipment back in place
Time to head back to base
They went back via the Westgate Run
To ogle the women and a bit of banter and fun
While in the back Johnny did expound
Which type of computers could be found
For those with limited capability
A computer to match their ability
Of which there was a choice
Even one activated by voice
Just say "Open windows" Johnny did tell
"Clever" said Oaksey "does it open the drapes as
well?"

Trev Wainwright
Castleford, West Yorkshire, United Kingdom

*Based on a true conversation that took place among
the crew of a Fire Engine returning to base.*

Talking to Fear
     after Denise Levertov, *Talking to Grief*

The Wawel Dragon is a famous mythological
dragon in Polish folklore

Fear, you are as the Wawel Dragon,
an oppressive reptile living
in the cave of my stomach;
your large bones crush against my ribs.
I don't want you.
If I hunt you,
wrestle you in your own lair,
pin you down,
stuff your fiery mouth with snow,
will this end you?
You think I don't know you want my peace
as an offering of appeasement.
You think I don't know your real desire is
the tender maiden of my heart. You need
its innocence.
You need the way it freely opens
like a lost lamb,
easily devoured.
But it knows pain.
Pain is the greater fire.
You are a dwindling kindle.

Loretta Diane Walker
Odessa, Texas

Pyro Genesis

Fire scorches friend and foe, virtue & vice
indiscriminately, still St Peter doppelgängers—
apostolic pandemic deniers—encourage questionable,
closed, colosseum behavior, make sword swallowers
digest blazing torches esophagus bound, feverish,
haunting, voices crying, *"Defy the Danger!"*

Fire purifies wanton acts & desires
ignites feeble clarity with benevolent sparks
yet both treasures & trash combust alike, bursting
into a sanctified holocaust of flames moving…,
growing…, moving…, growing like a backdraft
sucking fresh air from oxygen rich rooms.

Fire consumes normalcy, a fuel friendly concept,
fortune's flare-ups mesh like fish-net stockings,
fashion an inferno out of superior thoughts &
inferior design, both lost in charred passageways
along dead-end quests to restore the status quo,
engender burnt gifts—uncontested opportunity.

Fire simmers below aqua skies beholding earth's
scorched flesh & ribs, an exhausted funeral pyre,
hallowed foundation to transform, rebuild seared
granite stone & smoldering ashes, order evolving
flickering promises intensified, re-imagined,
realized on social unrest's heels as cinders cool.

Sterling Warner
Union, Washington

a letter a day keeps depression away

I like to close my love letters with a wax seal
as my wax stick is depositing the
boiling drops onto the envelope
the flame nearly scorches my fingertips.

in this moment I realize I am willing to burn myself
in order to make something beautiful
I am willing to burn myself in the hopes
that someone will love me.

Abbie Williams
Hewitt, Texas

Fire, Flames, and Fury

CONFLAGRATIONS ON OUR STREETS
Some say it is purgation/a cleansing flame
Others cannot stand the heat.
Fire burns as well as heals.
Warmth of a mother's love.
Heat-seeking missiles of criticism
Volcanic as temper tantrum lava.
Cool down,man! CHILL...
But the whole world is warming!
Icebergs /glaciers melting
The heat is on.
The Fire Next Time. James Baldwin.
Robert Frost inaugurates.
We are made of water and the waters are boiling.
Pele/Vulcan-old gods of fire and of flame resurrect.
They wish to claim land as sand /desert.
Temperatures rise in swollen Summers.
Water Wars. Emotional droughts.
The lick of fires burned Australia (and
Siberia/California)
Amazon burns.
Smoke from Mexico fires crosses Borders illegally.
SMOG ALERT!
This may be an Age of Fire.
Cool it, Man!
You are BURNING UP!

Thom Woodruff
Austin, Texas

ember

she awakes
house afire
smoke licking
caressing her skin
through the satin gown
as she floats
down the hall
to the baby's room,
already ablaze.
lost.

now she spends
antiseptic hours
clothed in gauze
and ointments.
for a long time
she will not kiss
or be kissed.

but the fire inside her
cannot understand this,
continues to smolder
at fever pitch.
needs to take a lover.

Christopher Woods
Chappell Hill, Texas

Fuel

An odd tree: its six trunks
look as if it had been coppiced
when the offices were built
some sixty years ago.

Under full sail, the summer gale
felled one trunk across the road,
revealing the rottenness at its base.
The Council's men sawed it
into logs for stoves
and lopped thinner boughs
threatening passers-by,
leaving the waste to dry
on the offices' fronting sward.

Come November, perhaps,
this unsellable dead wood
will once more reach skywards –
as flames, on Bonfire Night.

Mantz Yorke
Manchester, United Kingdom

Burning Bush

We are all
That burning bush
Knowing that
Having been created
We will not be consumed

Alight with passion
Full of inconsistent
Pain and suffering
Each of us a unique being

Part of the great dance
Each step essential
To that holy ground
Sanctifying everything

Surrounded by angels
Who remind us
That who we are
Is enough

Marilyn Zwicker
Austin, Texas

Waco Cultural Arts Fest 2020

Doreen Ravenscroft, festival director
Sandi Horton, WordFest chairperson

Details about **WordFest** can be found on our Facebook page
at **www.facebook.com/wacoartsfest.org**

Information about the **Waco Cultural Arts Fest** can be found
at **www.wacoartsfest.org**, or on Facebook page at
www.facebook.com/WacoCulturalArtsFestival.

Thank you to our WordFest sponsors and affiliates!

Cultural Arts of Waco

Creative Waco

City of Waco

Waco Convention Center

Texas Commission of the Arts

National Endowment of the Arts

Austin International Poetry Festival